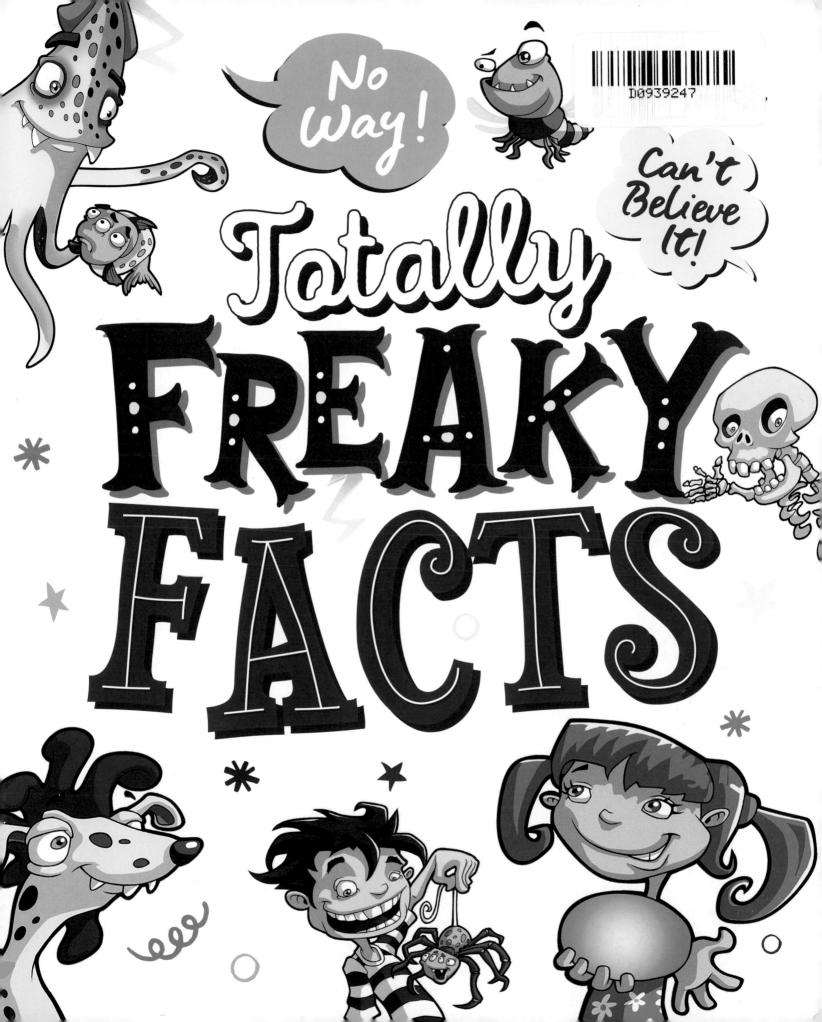

Silver Dolphin Books
An imprint of Printers Row Publishing Group
A division of Readerlink Distribution Services, LLC.
10350 Barnes Canyon Road, Suite 100, San Diego,
CA 92121
www.silverdolphinbooks.com

Printers Row Publishing Group is a division of Readerlink Distribution
Services, LLC.
Silver Dolphin Books is a registered trademark of Readerlink
Distribution Services, LLC.

All notations of errors or omissions should be addressed to Silver
Dolphin Books, Editorial Department, at the above address. All other
correspondence (author inquiries, permissions) concerning the
content of this book should be addressed to:
Hinkler Books Pty Ltd
45-55 Fairchild Street
Heatherton Victoria 3202 Australia
www.hinkler.com

Written by Nick Bryant and Katie Hewat
Illustrated by Glen Singleton
Cover Design by Hinkler Studio
Typeset by MPS Limited

ISBN: 978-1-68412-593-7

Manufactured, printed, and assembled in Heshan, Guangdong, China.
First printing, February 2019. LP/02/19
23 22 21 20 19   1 2 3 4 5

Contents

No Way!

Can't Believe It!

Unusual ANIMAL FACTS

The only bird that can fly backward is the hummingbird.

The giant squid has the largest eyes in the world.

There's always one stray hummingbird in the flock who's got to show he can fly backward.

HHMMM HMMM HHMMM HMMM

I'm sure I've never been down this end of the tank before !! Better go explore the new territory at the other end of the tank !

Goldfish can grow up to 23 in long and weigh over 6 lbs.

A rat can survive longer without water than a camel.

Toupées for dogs are sold in Tokyo.

A dolphin sleeps with one eye open.

A crocodile cannot stick its tongue out.

A mammal's blood is red, an insect's blood is yellow, and a lobster's blood is blue.

Loud, fast music makes termites chew faster.

A blue whale's tongue weighs more than an elephant.

An ostrich's eye is bigger than its brain.

Bats always exit a cave to the left.

Domestic cats kill an estimated one billion wild birds each year in the U.S.

Tigers have striped *skin*, not just striped fur.

The scene at the entrance to the bat cave at rush hour.

Terry had to be careful in locker rooms. For he had a secret. He was different from all the other tigers at school. Instead of stripes on his skin, ... Terry had spots!

The blue whale's whistle is the loudest noise made by an animal.

The heart of a giraffe weighs more than 25 lbs, is 2 ft wide, and has walls 3 in thick.

Camels have three eyelids to protect their eyes from sand.

A mole can dig a tunnel over 300 ft long in just one night.

Elephants are not afraid of mice.

Even though a blind mole can dig a tunnel up to 300 feet long...that doesn't mean it knows where it's digging to!

Slugs have four noses.

It is estimated that 25 percent of cat owners blow-dry their pets.

Elephants are not afraid of mice, but are very afraid of the similar-looking Rogue Rwandan Rock-hopping Rodent.

HI JUMBO!

Only female mosquitoes bite.

Snakes are immune to their own venom.

Don't tell me! It must have been the wash... the trim...the conditioner... and the BLOW DRY. Am I right?

Even though it could grow up to 9 ft tall, the stegosaurus had a brain that was only around the size and roughly the shape of a bent hotdog.

The fastest bird is the peregrine falcon. It can fly faster than 190 miles per hour.

In the Caribbean, mangrove oysters "climb trees"; when high tide comes in, they get pushed against the trunks and attach themselves. When the tide moves out, they're left clinging to the bark!

If an axolotl, an amphibian, loses a limb it can grow it back. This is called regeneration.

Cats cannot taste sweet things.

Cymothoa exigua is a small crustacean that eats the tongue of a fish, and then pretends to *be* the tongue! It attaches itself to the fish's mouth and helps itself to the fish's food.

Herons have been observed dropping insects on the water, then catching the fish that surface to eat the insects.

The heron comes to the realization that if dropping insects on the water attracts teensy-weensy fish... it may also attract older, hungrier, not-so-friendly relatives.

When a mother cormorant, an aquatic bird, feels her offspring are ready to leave the nest, she makes sure this happens by destroying the nest completely.

The largest egg is laid by the ostrich. An ostrich egg can be 8 in in length and 6 in in diameter.

The smallest egg is laid by the hummingbird. Its egg is less than one third of an inch in diameter.

A blind chameleon is still able to change the color of its skin to match its environment.

Why you DON'T hear people saying... "At breakfast... I have my hummingbird egg... a piece of toast and jam and a cup of tea and I'm off to work for the day!"

OK..OK! Who's the wiseguy? I don't do that background!

Bald eagles can swim.

A zebra's skin is actually black. Their coat contains the black-and-white stripes.

The Goliath bird-eating tarantula from South America has a legspan of up to 11 in.

Hey! Did you see that show on TV last night about those bird-eating spiders they have in South America?

I did! I'm sure glad we don't live there!

Statistically you are more likely to be attacked by a cow than a shark.

An eagle can kill and carry an animal as large as a small deer.

At birth, a giant panda is smaller than a mouse.

A queen bee only uses her stinger to sting another queen bee.

An elephant's gestation period can be up to 22 months.

A chameleon's tongue is twice the length of its body.

To warn off enemies, the horned lizard squirts foul-tasting blood from its eyelids.

Spider silk, by weight, is stronger than steel.

A blue whale's heart only beats nine times per minute.

A hedgehog's heart beats 300 times per minute.

As this whale with a heart rate of only 9 beats per minute is about to smash my boat, do you think that it has the slightest concern about MY heart?

Horses can sleep standing up.

CLUNK

A cat needs four to five times more protein than a dog does.

When a baby kangaroo is born, it is only about 0.8 in long.

An electric eel can produce a shock of 600 volts. That's enough to knock a horse off of its feet.

Chimpanzees use tools more than any other animal except humans.

Lobsters can regenerate their legs, claws, and antennae if these parts are pulled off by a predator.

A bald eagle's nest can be 12 ft deep and 10 ft wide.

Parrots live longer than any other type of bird. There are reliable reports of parrots living to 150 years old.

An African elephant only chews with four teeth.

Flying fish actually glide on wind currents. They can glide 20 ft above the surface of the water.

Sea snakes are the most venomous snakes in the world.

A scallop swims by quickly clapping its shell open and shut. This makes a water jet that pushes the scallop along.

Some captive octopuses have learned to open jars containing food. Many aquariums now give their octopuses puzzles and other games to keep them from getting bored.

A fox will sometimes nip at the heels of cattle to make the cattle run. The cattle's stomping sends mice and other rodents out of the ground for the fox to eat.

Lungfish can live out of water for as long as four years.

Polar bears have been known to swim up to 62 miles without stopping.

An ant can lift 10 times its own weight.

The Egyptian vulture eats ostrich eggs. It uses stones to crack the eggshell.

Salamanders breathe through their skin.

Farmers in England are required by law to provide their pigs with toys.

A rhinoceros' horn is made mainly of keratin—just like human hair and nails.

A woodpecker can peck up to 20 times per second.

Kiwi birds mate for life. This can be for up to 30 years.

Before seahorse eggs hatch, the male seahorse carries them in a pouch on his stomach.

A shark does not have bones. Its skeleton is made of cartilage.

Squirrels have many memory tricks that help them find their hidden stashes of food.

The stegosaurus had a brain the size of a lime.

An octopus has three hearts.

The praying mantis is the only insect that can turn its head.

A penguin can drink saltwater because it has a gland in its throat that removes the salt from the water.

There are more plastic flamingos in the USA than real ones.

A giraffe has the same number of vertebrae in its neck as a mouse.

Turkeys often look up at the sky during a rainstorm. Unfortunately, some have drowned as a result.

The Loch Ness monster is a protected animal under Scottish law.

A monkey was made a corporal in the South African army during World War II.

A snail can sleep for three years.

An adult bear can run as fast as a horse.

Sheep can recognize other sheep from photographs.

A locust can eat its own weight in food in one day. A typical person eats their weight in food in about six months.

Bees have five eyes.

Sharks kill approximately 40 people each year. This is a tiny number compared to the number of people that drown each year: around 360,000.

Hornets, wasps, and bees kill more people in the U.S. than venomous snakes, causing around 60 deaths per year.

Baby elephants suck their trunks for comfort, just like human babies suck their thumbs.

Mosquito repellents do not repel. The repellent blocks a mosquito's sense of smell so it does not know a person is nearby.

A zebra foal can run with the herd only an hour after its birth!

A marine catfish has taste buds on the outside of its body.

A polar bear's fur is not white, but transparent.

Some locusts have an adult lifespan of only a few weeks, after having lived in the ground as grubs for 15 years.

After living in a hole for 15 years, I'm hungry enough to eat all the plants in the world.

Butterflies taste with their feet.

Fleas that live on rats have probably killed more people than anything else because they spread the bubonic plague.

Hi. What do you plan to do today?

Oh.. perhaps I'll go off and bite a couple of unsuspecting people ...pass on the Black Death ...wipe out half of Europe.

The sixth American President John Quincy Adams owned a pet alligator. He kept it in the East Room of the White House.

All worker ants are female.

A cockroach can live up to one week with its head cut off before it dies of dehydration.

Dogs can make about 10 vocal sounds. Cats can make more than 100 vocal sounds.

Walruses turn pink when basking in the sun, as blood vessels closest to the surface of the skin fill up.

More animals are killed by cars each year than by hunters.

A beaver can hold its breath underwater for up to 15 minutes.

There are 340 breeds of dog recognized globally.

Vultures have a unique defense mechanism: they vomit on their enemies.

Wombats have cube-shaped poop—and lots of it! A wombat can poop from 80 to 100 cubes each night.

Platypuses swim with their eyes, ears, and nostrils closed.

Cockroaches could survive a nuclear holocaust because radiation does not affect them as much as it affects other species.

The embryos of tiger sharks fight each other while in their mother's womb. Only the survivors are born.

Some lizards use their lungs to help them hear. Sound makes the lizard's chest vibrate. The vibrations are carried by air from the lungs to the lizard's head where they are heard.

Orangutans protect their territory by burping loudly to warn off intruders.

Frogs can vomit. A frog vomits its stomach first, so that its stomach is dangling out of its mouth. Then the frog uses its forearms to dig out the stomach's contents. Then the frog swallows its stomach again.

Australian earthworms can grow up to 10 ft in length.

Elephants and humans are the only animals that can stand on their heads.

Not content with being able to stand on his head... Eric the elephant attempted more difficult gymnastic exercises with disastrous consequences.

There is enough poison in a poison-dart frog to kill 10 people.

A camel can drink up to 30 gallons of water at one time.

Rats and horses cannot vomit.

Racehorses can wear out new horseshoes in just one race.

Minnows have teeth in their throat.

If a seastar loses a limb, it can regrow a new one in its place!

A dolphin can hear sound underwater from 15 miles away.

A scallop has 35 eyes.

Some chimpanzees and orangutans have been taught human sign language.

Most insects are deaf.

Capuchin monkeys wash by peeing on their hands and rubbing it over their bodies.

Snails produce a sticky discharge that forms a protective layer under them as they crawl. The discharge is so effective that a snail can crawl along the edge of a razor blade without cutting itself.

Earthworms have five hearts.

All pet hamsters are descended from one female found with her young in the wild in 1930.

Some reptiles, such as chameleons, have eyes that operate independently of each other, so that the animal can see in two directions at once.

Groups of sea otters tie themselves together with kelp so they do not drift apart while they sleep.

A camel's hump stores fat, not water.

Neither emus nor kangaroos can walk backward.

Cats hate the smell of citrus fruits.

The tusks of the woolly mammoth were 16 ft long.

A group of crows is called a murder.

Camels will spit if annoyed.

The saltwater crocodile has the world's strongest bite—more than 20 times stronger than a human's.

Ninety-One FUNNY PHOBIAS

Ablutophobia is the fear of bathing.

Acarophobia is the fear being infested with tiny bugs.

Agyrophobia is the fear of streets or crossing the street.

Alektorophobia is the fear of chickens.

Bob's irrational fear of chickens even went as far as the 5 PIECE CHICKEN MEAL DEAL (with a FREE DRINK)...at the local fast-food restaurant

Alliumphobia is the fear of garlic.

Amensiphobia is the fear of amnesia.

Anablephobia is the fear of looking up.

Anemophobia is the fear of wind.

Apeirophobia is the fear of eternity.

Arachibutyrophobia is the fear of peanut butter sticking to the roof of the mouth.

Arnold's fear of looking up eventually became his undoing...

I don't like the look of that shadow...! Without looking up...I think it looks like a .....

Automysophobia is the fear of being dirty.

I think I have a fear of being dirty!

How are you going to handle that? You're a pig! Pigs love mud!

Barophobia is the fear of gravity.

Basiphobia is the fear of walking or falling.

Bibliophobia is the fear of books.

Bogyphobia is the fear of the Boogeyman.

STINK? Not me! I have no fear of body odor! Those sort of things don't worry me! I might drive around in a hot delivery truck all day lifting boxes, but I'm always as fresh as a daisy!

Bromidrosiphobia is the fear of body odor.

Chaetophobia is the fear of hair.

Chrometophobia is the fear of money.

Chronophobia is the fear of time.

Clinophobia is the fear of going to bed.

Coimetrophobia is the fear of cemeteries.

Coulrophobia is the fear of clowns.

Cyberphobia is the fear of computers or technology.

Cyclophobia is the fear of bicycles.

Decidophobia is the fear of making decisions.

Doraphobia is the fear of fur.

Ecophobia is the fear of home.

Emetophobia is the fear of vomiting.

Geniophobia is the fear of chins.

Genuphobia is the fear of knees.

Geumaphobia is the fear of taste.

Gnosiophobia is the fear of knowledge.

Gymnophobia is the fear of being naked.

Heliophobia is the fear of the sun.

Ideophobia is the fear of ideas.

Kleptophobia is the fear of stealing or being stolen from.

Koinoniphobia is the fear of rooms full of people.

Koniophobia is the fear of dust.

Lachanophobia is the fear of vegetables.

Leukophobia is the fear of the color white.

Logophobia is the fear of words.

Lutraphobia is the fear of otters.

Macrophobia is the fear of long waits.

Meteorophobia is the fear of meteors.

I have a terrible fear of being hit by a meteor from space. But the scientists tell us there's only a one in a trillion chance of one hitting someone... so I don't know what I'm worrying about!

Microphobia is the fear of small things.

Mnemophobia is the fear of memories.

Myrmecophobia is the fear of ants.

Mythophobia is the fear of myths or false statements.

Myxophobia is the fear of slimy things.

Nebulaphobia is the fear of fog.

Fearing a thick fog entering his living room and engulfing him while sleeping in front of the TV... ...Harold closed all doors and windows...but failed to close Harry the cat's cat flap in the back door.

Nephophobia is the fear of clouds.

Nomatophobia is the fear of names.

Numerophobia is the fear of numbers.

Ochophobia is the fear of vehicles.

A fear of vehicles drove Shirley to start a movement to bring back the HORSE for transport.

HORSE POWER is great! BRING BACK THE HORSE!

Give JOBS to out of work HORSES

I've been unemployed standing around eating grass in a paddock for five years!

Ombrophobia is the fear of rain.

Ommetaphobia is the fear of eyes.

Ornithophobia is the fear of birds.

Pagophobia is the fear of ice or frost.

Papaphobia is fear of the Pope.

Papyrophobia is the fear of paper.

Due to his irrational fear of rain, Alex spent two days pinned to a wall under an awning waiting for the low pressure storm to leave.

Paraskavedekatriaphobia is the fear of Friday the 13th.

Pedophobia is the fear of children.

AHHHHH KIDS!

Peladophobia is the fear of baldness.

Phagophobia is the fear of swallowing.

Philophobia is the fear of falling in love.

Esmerelda's fear of love was thinly disguised as a lack of interest.

Phonophobia is the fear of loud sounds.

Plutophobia is the fear of wealth.

Pogonophobia is the fear of beards.

Pteronophobia is the fear of being tickled with feathers.

Ranidaphobia is the fear of frogs.

Rupophobia is the fear of dirt.

Samhainophobia is the fear of Halloween.

Selenophobia is the fear of the moon.

Somniphobia is the fear of sleep.

Symmetrophobia is the fear of symmetry.

Syngenesophobia is the fear of relatives.

Taphephobia is the fear of being buried alive.

Telephonophobia is the fear of telephones.

Tonsurephobia is the fear of haircuts.

Tremophobia is the fear of trembling.

Tropophobia is the fear of moving or change.

Uranophobia is the fear of heaven or the sky.

Vestiphobia is the fear of clothing.

Vitricophobia is the fear of stepfathers.

Xanthophobia is the fear of the color yellow.

Xenophobia is the fear of strangers or foreigners.

Zelophobia is the fear of jealousy.

Zemmiphobia is the fear of the mole rat.

Zoophobia is the fear of animals.

And finally…

Phobophobia is the fear of fear.

Panophobia is the fear of everything.

George hid under his pillow when his fear of everything got to him…

If I could move my jaws to say it... I'd say... "–129...Hey that's pretty cold!"

VOSTOK, ANTARTICA, JULY 21, 1983

The coldest temperature recorded on Earth was –129°F at Vostok, Antarctica, on July 21, 1983.

Charles Osborne had the hiccups for 68 years.

The world record for most jumps on a pogo stick is 206,864.

Bhutan was the last country to get the telephone. It did not have one until 1981.

The world's largest iceberg, found in 2000 and named B-15, had a surface area of around 4,200 square miles—that's bigger than the island of Jamaica!

The tallest tree in the world, a coast redwood, is 379.7 ft tall.

The record for the most one-handed back handsprings in a row is 34.

The biggest palace in the world is the Imperial Palace in Beijing. It has so many rooms that you could sleep in a different room every night for 25 years.

The longest trip in a wave-powered boat was 4,350 nautical miles.

Although covered with ice, Antarctica is the driest place on the planet, with a humidity lower than the Gobi Desert.

For 110 years, the USA was the world's top manufacturing nation. It was overtaken by China in 2010.

The longest time spent standing on one foot is 76 hours, 40 minutes.

The record for the oldest female performing flying trapeze artist was set in 2017 by 84-year-old Betty Goedhart in San Diego, California.

The biggest pumpkin in the world weighed 2,624 lbs. It was grown in Germany.

The highest jump by a dog was achieved by a pup named Feather in Frederick, Maryland. Feather jumped 75.5 inches high!

The person with the longest nose ever recorded was Thomas Wedders. His nose measured 7.5 in. Thomas worked in a freak show in the 1770s.

The longest place name is "Bangkok" in Thai. It is: Krungthep Mahanakhon Bovorn Ratanakosin Mahintharayutthaya Mahadilokpop Noparatratchathani Burirom Udomratchanivet Mahasathan Amornpiman Avatarnsathit Sakkathattiyavisnukarmprasit. It means "City of Angels." It is usually shortened to Krungthep Mahanakhon, for obvious reasons.

The record for the most scorpions held in the mouth at one time is 22.

The first automobile race in the USA was held in Chicago in 1895. The track ran from Chicago to Evanston, Illinois. The winner was J. Frank Duryea, whose average speed was 7.5 miles per hour.

The largest crater on the moon is also the largest known impact crater in the solar system. It measures 1,550 miles across.

Strongman John Evans holds the world record for the heaviest weight balanced only on his head. He balanced 101 bricks that weighed 416 lbs.

The fastest wind speed recorded was 318 miles per hour in Oklahoma on May 3, 1999.

T.J. loses his best kite in 318-mile winds... somewhere over Oklahoma in 1999.

Shoot... That was a good kite too!

The largest known volcano is Olympus Mons on Mars. It is 370 miles wide and 79,000 ft tall. It is almost three times taller than Mount Everest.

The Holy See, or the State of the Vatican City, in Rome, Italy, is the smallest sovereign state in the world. It has a population of less than 1,000 people.

The largest pearl ever found weighed 75 lbs.

The youngest college graduate ever got his bachelor's degree in 1994 at the age of 10 years, 5 months.

Dorothy Straight's first book, *How The World Began*, was written in 1954 when she was just four years old; it was later published in 1964, making her the youngest female author to write a published book.

The most powerful computer in the world is the Summit supercomputer at Oak Ridge National Laboratory in Tennessee. It can do 200 trillion calculations per second, which translates to 200 petaflops per second.

The largest Hula-Hoop ever spun was 16 ft, 10 in in diameter.

Jon Brower Minnoch weighed in at 1,400 lbs when he was admitted to the hospital, making him the heaviest person ever recorded. Minnoch was discharged at 476 lbs.

The tallest living man in the world is Sultan Kösen, who is a towering 8 ft, 2.8 in tall.

The loudest burp was 109.9 decibels.

The record for holding one's breath underwater is 24 minutes.

The record for the most apples bobbed in one minute is 37.

Neil Harbisson of the UK holds the record for being the first person to have an antenna implanted in their skull, which he had attached in 2004. It can receive phone calls and access the Internet.

Golf is the only sport that has been played on the moon.

The shortest war in history was fought between Zanzibar and England in 1896. The war had lasted for just 38 minutes when Zanzibar surrendered.

The longest recorded flight of a chicken is 13 seconds.

The world's smallest tree is the dwarf willow. It grows to 2 inches on the tundra of Greenland.

A Greenlander about to flatten a whole forest of dwarf willows in one step!

The world's largest collection of snow globes belongs to Wendy Suen of China. She owns 4,059 globes.

The oldest known living thing is a Great Basin bristlecone pine located in the White Mountains on the California-Nevada border. The tree is estimated to be over 5,000 years old.

Chucky brings home the 5,000-year-old Bristlecone pine after a hiking trip to the White Mountains of USA.

The *Guinness Book of Records* holds the record for being the book most often stolen from public libraries.

The farthest flight ever made on a hoverboard was 1.4 miles by Franky Zapata of France.

Flight attendant Vesna Vulović of Yugoslavia fell 33,330 ft from an airplane into a snowy forest in Srbská Kamenice, Czechoslovakia, on January 26, 1972. It was the longest fall a person has survived.

It's ONLY NATURAL

Watermelons are grown square in Japan so that they take up less space and are easier to stack.

After 20 years of trying to stack round watermelons unsuccessfully in a Japanese fruit market...Hiroshi hits on a great idea.

From now on I'll grow square watermelons that I can stack really high!

An apple, potato, and onion all taste sweet if you eat them with your nose plugged.

Jupiter is bigger in mass than all of the other planets in our solar system combined.

If you plug your nose while you eat it... an onion tastes just like an apple! Hey it saves on buying apples!

Hot water takes up more room than cold water.

Natural gas has no smell. The smell is added for safety reasons.

Swiss scientists have found that gently rubbing the leaves of plants can make them healthier.

Strawberries contain more vitamin C than oranges.

Forty-one percent of the Moon is not visible from Earth at any time.

No son, There's nobody on the moon. It's just a big hunk of dry rock revolving around the Earth that shines brightly at night.

Yes Captain Zardok ...we're ready to invade Earth on your command!

WHAT REALLY HAPPENS ON THE FORTY ONE PERCENT OF THE MOON WE CAN'T SEE FROM EARTH.

Because of the change in gravity, you'd only weigh $\frac{1}{6}$ of your current weight on the moon.

A blue moon is a term for the second full moon within a single calendar month.

The age of the universe is 13.75 billion years.

THE UNIVERSE TURNS 13·75 BILLION

The human body has 206 bones.

More than 90 percent of all organisms that have ever lived on Earth are extinct.

Sound travels through water four times faster than through air.

True berries include the grape, tomato, and eggplant, but not the raspberry or blackberry.

Pearls dissolve in vinegar.

The largest flower in the world is the corpse flower, or *Rafflesia*. It grows up to 4 ft wide and it stinks.

There are eight peas per pod on average.

In Calama, a town in the Atacama Desert of Chile, it has never rained.

Raindrops are not really shaped like drops; they are spherical.

Lemons contain more sugar than strawberries.

When scientists drilled through the ice of Antarctica's Lake Vanda, they discovered that the water at the bottom of the lake was an amazingly warm 77°F. Ice crystals heat the water by focusing light onto the bottom of the lake.

The Amazon rainforest makes $\frac{1}{5}$ of the world's oxygen.

The Antarctic ice sheet contains 90 percent of the world's fresh water.

A tomato is a fruit, not a vegetable.

Lettuce is part of the sunflower family.

Water is the only substance on Earth that is lighter as a solid than as a liquid.

Mercury is the only metal that is liquid at room temperature.

Antarctica is the only place on Earth that is not actually owned by any country. It is, in fact, administered under a treaty by 12 different countries.

Bananas are slightly radioactive, but you would have to eat around 10 million of them for the effect to be lethal.

Honey never spoils.

Australia is the only continent on Earth without an active volcano.

Fingernails grow nearly four times faster than toenails.

By raising your legs slowly and lying on your back, you can float instead of sinking in quicksand.

Scientists believe that the atmospheres of Uranus and Neptune contain enough pressure to crystallize carbon atoms, which means it may actually rain diamonds on these planets!

The apple, the almond, and the peach are all members of the rose family.

The average human produces from one to two quarts of saliva each day.

Venus and Uranus are the only planets that have a "backwards" rotation: from east to west.

On February 20, 1943, in a cornfield near the village of Paricutin, Mexico, the ground cracked open and began to spew red-hot rocks. A volcano was born. It grew to 35 ft the first day. By 1952, it had soared to 1,352 ft and had buried two towns.

The white oak does not produce acorns until it is about 50 years old.

GRUNCHING NUMBERS

Buckingham Palace has 775 rooms.

The opposite sides of a die always add up to seven.

Woodpecker scalps, porpoise teeth, and giraffe tails have all been used as money.

Scientists believe that the human nose can pick up around a trillion different smells.

Forty is the only number in English that, when spelled out, has all of its letters in alphabetical order.

There are more than 1,267 million telephone lines in the world.

The average office worker uses about 10,000 sheets of paper each year.

Twenty percent of all road accidents in Sweden involve a moose or elk.

There are more than 200 lashes on a human eyelid. Each lash is shed every three to five months.

More than 1,500 languages are spoken in Africa.

An ostrich egg takes an hour and a half to hard boil.

A porcupine has about 30,000 quills.

More than 80 billion tablets of aspirin are sold each year.

Humans have 650 muscles, but caterpillars have more than 4,000.

If you could drive to the sun at 55 miles per hour, it would take about 193 years.

A baby is born in the United States every seven seconds.

Sixty percent of the world's buttons are made in the Qiaotou factory in China.

Just 20 seconds' worth of fuel remained when *Apollo 11*'s lunar module landed on the moon.

All it took was a 20-second dispute over where to land to turn the first landing on the moon into the first crash on the moon!

Up to 10 inches of rain can fall on a rain forest in a single day.

A solar day on Mercury, from sunrise to sunset, lasts about six Earth months.

There are around 67 different types of bacteria that live in your belly button.

There are more than 40,000 varieties of rice.

Cats can spend 16 hours a day sleeping.

A bee needs to flap its wings 250 times per second to remain in the air.

Ninety-five percent of American adults own a cell phone.

After sleeping most of the day, Harry the Persian slept most of the night catching up on the sleep he missed during the day.

You can survive roughly three minutes without air, three days without water, and three weeks without food.

In the first eight months of his presidency, George W. Bush was on vacation 42 percent of the time.

An alligator has 80 teeth.

It takes approximately 540 peanuts to make a standard 12 oz jar of peanut butter.

Negative-forty degrees is the only temperature that is the same in Fahrenheit and Celsius.

The Great Wall Of China is 3,890 miles long.

Summer and winter on Uranus each last 21 Earth years.

Fifty Bibles are sold every minute.

There are roughly five million active stamp collectors in the United States.

There is a McDonald's in 101 countries.

Many people around the world believe that the number 13 is unlucky, which is why many buildings do not have a 13th floor.

There are 2.5 million rivets in the Eiffel Tower.

The Earth travels around the Sun at about 67,000 miles per hour.

The burrowing rate of the gopher is equivalent to a human digging a tunnel 18 inches wide and 7 miles long in 10 hours.

Close to four billion movie tickets are sold in India every year.

One in five children in the world has never been inside a classroom.

One ragweed plant can release one billion grains of pollen per year.

On average, 100 acres of pizza are eaten every day in the USA.

A mayfly lives for one day.

There are more insects in a one square mile of rural land than there are people on the planet.

DON'T MOVE SHIRLEY OLD GIRL! Do you realize that if you do.... you might squash more bugs than there are people in China!

The largest American bill ever printed was for $100,000.

Roman numerals do not have a number zero.

A dairy cow will give about 350,000 glasses of milk in its lifetime.

Chamoy Thipyaso was convicted of fraud and sentenced to 141,078 years in a Thai prison.

The digits in multiples of nine always add up to nine.

The first product to have its barcode scanned was a pack of Wrigley's gum.

An icosagon is a shape with 20 sides.

One 75-watt bulb gives off more light than three 25-watt bulbs.

Twenty thousand men took 22 years to build the Taj Mahal.

Bolivia has two capital cities: La Paz and Sucre.

The American government holds nearly three percent of all the gold refined through history. Most of it is at Fort Knox.

A Weddell seal can hold its breath underwater for an hour.

In America, every major league baseball team buys about 20,000 baseballs a year.

The height of the Eiffel Tower varies by as much as 6 inches, depending on the temperature.

Mickey Mouse received 800,000 pieces of fan mail in 1933.

MICKEY MOUSE READS HIS FAN MAIL

The blue whale, the largest animal ever, can grow up to 100 ft long. It weighs as much as four large dinosaurs, 23 elephants, 230 cows, or 1,800 men.

About 10 percent of all people are left-handed.

Almost one quarter of all mammal species on Earth are bats.

Bats make up one quarter of all mammals on Earth...
And Juan finds the cave in Bolivia where they all live.

Lightning is five times hotter than the surface of the sun.

The average American over 50 will have spent five years waiting in lines.

The Earth is 4.54 billion years old.

The search engine Google got its name from the word "googol," which is the number one with a hundred zeros after it.

The largest hotel in the world is the First World Hotel in Malaysia. It has 7,351 rooms.

Wearing headphones can increase the bacteria in your ears.

The leaves of the Amazon water lily can be 8 ft wide.

It takes about 63,000 trees to make the Sunday edition of the *New York Times*.

It takes nearly 3,000 cows to supply the USA's National Football League with enough leather to make a year's supply of footballs.

In Haiti, only 12 out of every 1,000 people own a car.

Pain travels through the human body at a speed of over 350 ft per second.

The Sun makes up 99 percent of the matter in our solar system.

Around 70 percent of the oxygen in the atmosphere is created by marine plants.

The average person spends three years of their life on the toilet.

There are approximately 3,500 astronomers in the United States, but more than 15,000 astrologers.

The average number of aircraft in the sky at any given time is 5,000.

After hearing that a person drinks 20,000 gallons of water in a lifetime... Arnold decided to drink all of his share in one go and get it over with.

A person drinks about 20,000 gallons of water in their lifetime.

The human skull contains 22 bones.

Lightning strikes the Earth 100 times every second.

You share your birthday with more than 19 million people.

One bat can consume 1,000 mosquitoes in a single hour.

An office desk has 400 times more bacteria on it than a toilet does.

The average lead pencil can be used to draw a line 35 miles long or to write approximately 50,000 English words.

30 miles into his 35-mile line Al's pencil began to run low... But fortunately for Al he had a spare pencil to finish the last 5 miles of his line. And why was he drawing a 35-mile line? Well... it was easier than writing 50,000 words...

By weight, a hamburger costs more than a new car.

No piece of dry, square paper can be folded in half more than seven times.

More than 14 billion pencils are manufactured each year in the world. If these were placed end to end, they would circle the world 62 times.

Recycling one tin can saves enough energy to power a television for three hours.

If all the blood vessels in your body were placed end to end, they would make a line about 60,000 miles long.

In one day your heart beats 115,200 times.

At a steady jogger's pace of 6 miles per hour, it would take 173 days to go around the equatorial circumference of Earth, and more than 5 years to go around Jupiter, the largest planet.

OUCH! It's my sore toe. I can't go on!

Herb was forced to abandon his 173 day training run around the world after only 10 minutes blaming an ingrown toenail as the reason. His coach and manager feared his problem toe may act up on his 5-year run around the planet Jupiter.

The Empire State Building consists of more than 10 million bricks.

The longest conga line had 119,986 people in it.

There are more than 4,500 living species of cockroaches.

After the dust had settled... King Kong counted some of the 10 million bricks that once made up the Empire State Building.

A hummingbird's heart can beat more than 1,200 times per minute.

A human's small intestine is 20 ft long.

Scientists estimate that there are at least 15 million stars for every person on Earth.

A car traveling at 100 miles per hour would take more than 29 million years to reach the nearest star beyond the sun.

Is it much further to this star? The kids are getting restless and need lunch. I know it's going to take 29 million years to get there... but don't speed! You're already doing 100!

There are twenty-four cities and towns named Hollywood in the United States.

One species of bamboo can grow up to 35 inches in one day.

It is estimated that 6,500 languages are spoken in the world today.

India has over 150,000 post offices.

You blink over 10 million times in a year.

The most drought-resistant tree is the baobab tree. It can store 4,000 liters of water in its trunk for later use.

It was while chopping firewood in the Outback that Jack discovered the difference between a gum tree and a Baobab tree is about 4,000 liters of water.

Halley's Comet passes the Earth every 75–76 years. It will pass again in the year 2061.

Rats multiply so quickly that, in 18 months, two rats could have more than one million descendants.

A butterfly has more than 12,000 lenses in each eye.

There are more cell phones than people in the United States.

The combined wealth of the world's 250 richest people is greater than the combined wealth of the poorest 1.5 billion people.

The first license plates were introduced in 1901.

Outer space begins 50 miles above the Earth.

When awake, cats spend up to 30 percent of their time grooming.

Rex was not content with the average 30% of his time spent grooming... He went for the full 100%

A woodchuck breathes only 10 times per hour while hibernating. An active woodchuck breathes 2,100 times per hour.

An elephant can smell water nearly 3 miles away.

Linen can absorb up to 20 times its weight in moisture before it feels damp.

During a typical human life, a heart will beat approximately 2.5 billion times.

In 1956, 80 percent of American households had a refrigerator compared to only 8 percent of British households.

A hippopotamus can open its mouth 4 ft wide.

The sperm whale's intestines are over 450 ft long.

There are around six sheep for every one person in New Zealand.

Each year lightning starts about 10,000 fires in the United States.

Each year in the United States, chickens lay 79 billion eggs.

A human sneeze exits the mouth at almost 300 miles per hour. This is the speed of the wind in a class five tornado.

The French eat around 30,000 tons of snails every year.

The fastest moon in our solar system circles Jupiter once every seven hours. It travels faster than 70,000 miles per hour.

The largest jellyfish can grow up to 120 ft long.

A Boeing 747 airplane holds 57,285 gallons of fuel.

Besides inventing the telephone, Alexander Graham Bell set a world water speed record of 70 miles per hour in a hydrofoil boat.

The estimated number of M&Ms sold each day in the United States is 200 million.

There are approximately 31.5 million seconds in a year.

It takes 3 months to build a Rolls Royce and 17 hours to build a Toyota.

The moon has no atmosphere, so footprints left there by astronauts should remain for at least 10 million years.

The oldest fish in captivity lived to his mid-90s.

If you stretch out a standard Slinky, it measures 67 ft long.

Around seven percent of all the people who ever lived are alive today.

On average, 100 people choke to death on ballpoint pens every year.

There are 2,598,960 five-card hands possible in a 52-card deck of cards.

The cruise liner, the *Queen Elizabeth 2*, moves only 6 inches for each 1 gallon of diesel fuel that it burns.

Entertainment AND THE ARTS

Some Ancient Roman statues were made with detachable heads. That way, if the person after whom the statue was modeled became unpopular, the head could simply be removed and replaced with another.

James Cameron's film *Titanic* has spent the most consecutive weeks at number one at the box office.

The first time a toilet was shown on television was in the show *Leave It to Beaver*.

Look children! You've just got to see this! It's the first time it's been on television anywhere in the world. Do you see what it is? It's a TOILET!

Pablo Picasso's full name is: Pablo Diego José Francisco de Paula Juan Nepomuceno María de los Remedios Cipriano de la Santísima Trinidad Martyr Patricio Clito Ruíz y Picasso.

Charlie Chaplin once received 73,000 pieces of fan mail in three days.

Director George Lucas had trouble getting funding for the movie *Star Wars* because most film studios thought people would not go and see it.

No one knows where Mozart is buried.

Arnold Schwarzenegger was paid $15 million for saying only around 700 words in *Terminator 2: Judgment Day*.

The giant robotic T-Rex from *Jurassic Park* (1993) would occasionally come to life on its own on set, scaring the cast and crew. They later discovered that it was rain that caused it to malfunction.

English artist Andy Brown created a famous portrait of Queen Elizabeth II by sewing together 1,000 tea bags.

Barbie's full name is Barbara Millicent Roberts.

The first toy advertised on television was Mr. Potato Head.

Because metal was scarce, the Oscars given out during World War II were made of painted plaster.

Sherlock Holmes never said "Elementary, my dear Watson."

The most popular movie star in 1925 was the dog Rin Tin Tin.

Jon Voight is Angelina Jolie's father.

Soccer is the most popular sport in the world.

Pinocchio is Italian for "pine eyes."

"White Christmas" sung by Bing Crosby has sold over 100 million records, making it the most popular recording of all time.

In 1935, a writer named Dudley Nichols refused to accept the Oscar for his screenplay *The Informer* because the Writers' Guild was on strike.

The shortest television commercial was one quarter of a second long.

In 1970, George C. Scott refused the Best Actor Oscar for *Patton*.

In 1972, Marlon Brando refused the Oscar for his role in *The Godfather*.

In *Casablanca*, Humphrey Bogart never said "Play it again, Sam."

The world's most valuable guitar was a Gibson covered in diamonds and white gold. It sold for $2 million.

Barry Manilow won a Grammy Award for Best Song of the Year for his hit "I Write the Songs," but he didn't actually write the song.

Voice actor Frank Oz did the voices for many famous characters including Yoda, Miss Piggy, and Cookie Monster.

In Mel Brooks' *Silent Movie*, mime Marcel Marceau is the only person who has a speaking role.

The Bible has been translated into Klingon.

Boxing is the most popular theme in movies about sports.

Max makes a big mistake in believing the movie The Ring was going to be the horror film.

The world's longest-running play is *The Mousetrap*. It is a murder mystery that was written by Agatha Christie in 1947. It has been performed over 20,000 times.

In the 1991 Disney film *Beauty and the Beast*, one sign in the forest points to a place called Anaheim. Another sign points down a dark, sinister-looking path to Valencia. Anaheim is actually the site of Disneyland, while the rival Six Flags Magic Mountain amusement theme park is in the city of Valencia.

The first four countries to have television were England, the USA, the USSR, and Brazil.

THE DAY **BEFORE** TELEVISION STARTED IN BRITAIN

Donald Duck's middle name is Fauntleroy.

The song "Rudolph the Red-Nosed Reindeer" was invented in 1939 for a department store promotion.

Drew Barrymore shot to stardom at the age of six when she starred as Gertie in *E.T. the Extra-Terrestrial*.

Alfred Hitchcock did not have a belly button. It was eliminated when he was sewn up after surgery.

Virginia Woolf wrote many of her books at a standing desk.

Vincent van Gogh painted more than 30 self-portraits in less than four years.

Before the 1960s, men with long hair were not allowed to enter Disneyland.

One of the biggest box-office flops was Kevin Costner's *Waterworld*, which cost more than $200 million dollars to make.

Whoopi Goldberg's real name is Caryn Elaine Johnson.

Drew Carey once worked at Denny's.

The King of Hearts is the only king in a deck of cards without a mustache.

Mark Twain, one of America's best-loved authors, dropped out of school when he was 12 years old, after his father died.

Dolly Parton once lost a Dolly Parton look-alike contest.

In 1938, the creators of Superman sold the rights to the character for $130.

Justin Timberlake, Britney Spears, Christina Aguilera, and Ryan Gosling were all Mouseketeers on the *Mickey Mouse Club* TV show at the same time.

Vincent Van Gogh only sold one painting in his life.

There were 47 Charlie Chan movies. Six different actors played the role, but none of them were Chinese.

Pat Welsh was the voice of E.T.

More Monopoly money than real money is printed in a year.

The first time a toilet was flushed in a movie was in *Psycho*.

Sonny and Cher originally called themselves Caesar and Cleo.

The first episode of *Sesame Street* aired in 1969.

X-rays of the *Mona Lisa* show that there are three completely different versions, all painted by Leonardo da Vinci, under the final portrait.

X-Rays of the Mona Lisa reveal previous versions underneath!

Warren Beatty and Shirley Maclaine are brother and sister.

The sound effect of E.T. walking was made by someone squishing jelly in her hands.

Every time Beethoven sat down to write music, he poured cold water over his head.

The longest film without dialogue ever made was Andy Warhol's *Sleep*. It consists solely of a man sleeping for five hours.

The quietest piece of music in the world is John Cage's "4'33" which consists of a person sitting in front of a piano for 4 minutes and 33 seconds, then leaving.

Forty-eight pigs played the part of Babe in the movie of the same name.

The first CD pressed in the United States was Bruce Springsteen's *Born in the U.S.A.*

Beethoven wrote his famous Ninth Symphony after he was completely deaf.

In the Brothers Grimm version of *Snow White,* the seven dwarves do not have names. The names we know today, Doc, Sleepy, Sneezy, Happy, Grumpy, Dopey, and Bashful, were created by Disney for the 1937 film.

The people of Iceland read more books per capita than any other people in the world.

Lottie Dod was the youngest person ever to win a Wimbledon Ladies Singles Championship. She won the title in 1887 at age 15.

The first film with spoken dialogue premiered on October 6, 1927 in New York. It was *The Jazz Singer* starring Al Jolson.

John Travolta turned down the starring roles in *An Officer and a Gentleman* and *Forrest Gump*.

Whoopi Goldberg was a mortuary cosmetologist and a bricklayer before becoming an actress.

Leonardo da Vinci could write with one hand and draw with the other at the same time.

TAP TAP

It's well known that Leonardo Da Vinci could use both hands at the same time to write and draw... but he may have also been able to balance a small leather ball on his nose while tapping his foot to Italian folk tunes as well!

The oldest board game in the world is Senet, which originated in ancient Egypt around 3500BCE.

In most television commercials that show milk, a mixture of white paint and a little thinner is used in place of real milk. This is because cereal goes soggy and sinks to the bottom with real milk.

Humphrey Bogart was related to Princess Diana. They were seventh cousins.

The world's sixth-longest movie runs for 85 hours and is fittingly titled *The Cure for Insomnia*.

Bob fell asleep 84½ hours into the 85 hour movie... 'THE CURE FOR INSOMNIA' ...and missed the ending!

Seventy LUDICROUS LAWS

Many of these laws date back to a time when the ideals they represented were commonly accepted. Some are still in place today because the local authorities have not bothered to remove them yet.

Pacific Grove, California: It is a misdemeanor to kill or threaten a butterfly.

Ventura County, California: Cats or dogs cannot mate without a permit.

Sarasota, Florida: It is illegal to wear swimwear while singing in a public place.

Illinois: It is illegal to give lighted cigars to dogs, cats, or other pets.

Chicago, Illinois: A hatpin is considered a concealed weapon.

Florida: Men may not be seen publicly in any kind of strapless gown.

Belgium: Every child must learn the harmonica at elementary school.

Florida: If an elephant is left tied to a parking meter, the parking fee has to be paid.

Minnesota: It is illegal to mock skunks.

Michigan: It is illegal for a woman to cut her hair without her husband's consent.

Florida: Unmarried women are prohibited from parachuting on Sundays.

Alabama: It is illegal to wear a fake mustache that causes laughter in church.

Bellingham, Washington: It was once illegal for a woman to take more than three steps backward while dancing.

Brainerd, Minnesota: Every man must grow a beard.

Columbus, Ohio: It is illegal for stores to sell cornflakes on a Sunday.

Seattle, Washington: It is illegal to sell lollipops, but suckers are fine.

Virginia: All bathtubs must be outside, not in the house.

Here in Virginia... we have our bathtubs outside the house. We keep our towels inside the house. And that's where my towel is right now... inside the house... not out here where I need it! I wish I had a towel!

Toronto, Canada: It is illegal to ride streetcars on Sundays after eating garlic.

DING-DING DING-DING

TORONTO NEWS

POLICE

This is Sergeant Bottecelli from the Garlic Breath Squad. I'd like anyone who's eaten spaghetti sauce or garlic bread today to move outside and put your hands on the side of the streetcar... and not breathe on anybody please.

Arizona: You are allowed to win no more than 25 free games on a pinball machine.

Los Angeles, California: In 1838, a man had to obtain a license before serenading a woman.

Cleveland, Ohio: It is illegal to capture mice without a hunting license.

Arizona: It is illegal to hunt camels.

Kentucky: It is illegal to carry an ice cream cone in your pocket.

Louisiana: It is illegal to rob a bank, then shoot the teller with a water pistol.

Indiana: It is prohibited to take a bath in the winter.

Kentucky: You must take a bath at least once a year.

Alaska: It is illegal to look at or pursue a moose from a flying vehicle.

Atlanta, Georgia: It is illegal to tie a giraffe to a telephone pole or streetlight.

Idaho: It is forbidden to give a person a box of candy that weighs more than 50 lbs.

New York State: It is illegal to shoot a rabbit from a streetcar.

Somalia, Africa: It is illegal to carry old gum on the tip of your nose.

New Jersey: It is illegal to slurp soup.

Milan, Italy: Citizens can be fined $100 if seen in public without a smile on their face. Exemptions include time spent visiting patients in hospitals or attending funerals.

Dear Mabel,
Please wear these at all times! Only take them out for cleaning! Your loving Husband XX

Vermont: Women must obtain written permission from their husbands to wear false teeth.

Asheville, North Carolina: It is illegal to sneeze on city streets.

Oklahoma: People who make ugly faces at dogs may be fined and jailed.

Hello, POLICE? I'm a small white dog in trouble! Please send the DOG SQUAD around. I've got a man making faces at me who needs to go to jail!

California: It is illegal to eat a frog that has died during a frog-jumping contest.

Chicago, Illinois: It is illegal for a woman who weighs more than 200 lbs to ride a horse while wearing shorts.

San Francisco, California: It is illegal to use old underwear to clean cars in a car wash.

Thailand: It is illegal to step on money.

San Francisco, California: There is a ban on any mechanical device that reproduces obscene language.

Ancient Egypt: The penalty for killing a cat, even by accident, was death.

New York State: It is illegal to have a puppet show in your window.

San Francisco, California: Sneezing powders and stink bombs are prohibited.

New York State: It is illegal to let your dog sleep in the bathtub.

Mesquite, Texas: Young people are not allowed to have haircuts that are "startling or unusual."

Fairbanks, Alaska: It is illegal to give a moose a beer.

Washington State: Fake wrestling is not permitted.

KILLER and KARLA KOX the family wrestling team leave the emergency room after a wrestling match in Seattle.

Turkey: In the sixteenth and seventeenth centuries, anyone caught drinking coffee was put to death.

Russia: During the time of Peter the Great, any man who wore a beard had to pay a special tax.

Florida: It is illegal to doze off under a hair dryer.

Georgia: It is illegal to slap an old friend on the back.

Sgt. Smith kept mentioning it being illegal to nod off under a drier as Delores fought back sleep at the hairdresser's.

Missouri: It is illegal to play hopscotch on a Sunday.

Boston, Massachusetts: In the nineteenth century, it was illegal to bathe without a doctor's prescription.

Connecticut: It is illegal to walk across the street on your hands.

Avignon, France: It is illegal for a flying saucer to land in the city.

North Carolina: It is illegal to sell cotton lint or cotton seed at night.

A scene in the night sky over Avignon, France, where it's illegal for flying saucers to land....

You must understand. You cannot land here in our city of Avignon!

Go land in Paris instead!

AVIGNON

Switzerland: It was once against the law to slam your car door.

Gunther loses the very same door his wife slammed in an argument only ten minutes before in the fast lane of the motorway at 60 mph.

Athens, Greece: A driver's license can be taken away if the driver is deemed either unbathed or poorly dressed.

Hartford, Connecticut: It is illegal to plant a tree in the street.

Veronica left for work to find the "Set The Trees Free" organization had set two trees free illegally in her street.

Massachusetts: An old ordinance requires a person to have a permit to grow a goatee.

Florida: Housewives are not allowed to break more than three dishes a day.

Paraguay: Dueling is legal as long as both people are registered blood donors.

Amber...a housewife in Florida, smashes a week's worth of dishes in one go... leaving no dishes to smash tomorrow.

That's it! I'm going out to buy all my new plates in plastic!

Christiansburg, Virginia: It is illegal to spit.

Welcome to NORTH CAROLINA enjoy your stay!

Vernon held onto a spit right across the state of Virginia until he got to the border of North Carolina ...where he could spit freely.

Provincetown, Massachusetts: It is illegal to sell suntan oil before noon on a Sunday.

San Francisco California: It is illegal to beat a rug in front of your house.

Atwoodville, Connecticut: People cannot play Scrabble while waiting for a politician to speak.

New York State: It is illegal to do anything against the law.

Louisiana: Biting someone with your natural teeth is assault, while biting someone with your false teeth is aggravated assault.

Newark, New Jersey: Unless you have a doctor's note, it is illegal to buy ice cream after 6 p.m.

History NEVER REPEATS

Abraham Lincoln was an accomplished wrestler and has been honored by the Wrestling Hall of Fame.

The parachute was invented by Leonardo da Vinci in 1515.

Cleopatra was ethnically Greek, not Egyptian.

In 1867, the Russian Czar Alexander II sold Alaska for about $7.2 million to the United States. At the time, most people thought this was a really bad deal.

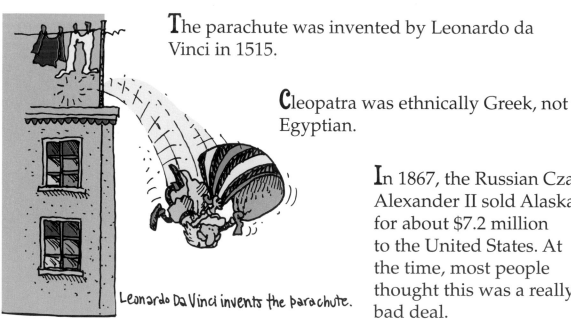

Leonardo Da Vinci invents the parachute.

In the Middle Ages, pepper was used for bartering, and it was often more valuable than gold.

The oldest restaurant still in business opened in Spain in 1725.

Early bagpipes were made from the stomachs of sheep.

In 1859 in Glamorgan, Wales, a shower of fish fell from the sky.

Napoleon constructed his battle plans in a sandbox.

Let's say this small wooden bucket is the Duke of Wellington. And this shovel is my army... ...And you....Well... you're just you I'm afraid...

Napoleon plans the Battle of Waterloo in a sandbox.

Hawaii officially joined the United States on August 21, 1959.

In nineteenth century Britain, you could be hung for writing graffiti on Westminster Bridge.

Athletes in the ancient Olympics competed in the nude.

Money made out of leather was once used in Russia.

The Japanese throne has been occupied by a member of the same family since the sixth century. The present emperor is the 125th in succession.

The umbrella originated in ancient Egypt, where it was used by the royal family and nobles as a symbol of rank.

The first vending machine was invented in Alexandria. It dispensed holy water.

The Roman Empire existed from about 750 BCE, when legend has it that Romulus and Remus founded Romeem to 1453 CE, when the Eastern, or Byzantine, branch of the Empire fell to the Turks.

The Vikings reached North America 500 years before the Pilgrims.

The Tower of London is currently the home of the British crown jewels. It has been a zoo, an observatory, a mint, and a prison.

The first product made by Sony was a rice cooker.

The dinosaurs were on Earth for almost 150 million years. That is 75 times longer than humans have been on the planet.

The Leaning Tower of Pisa has never been straight.

Before 1800, separate shoes for right and left feet were not designed.

I don't think these new left and right shoes will catch on. They're too hard to remember which one goes on which foot!

Edward tries out the first pair of left and right shoes in 1800.

The cigarette lighter was invented before the match.

Britain's youngest prime minister was William Pitt in 1783. He was 24 years old.

In 1916, Jeannette Rankin was the first woman elected to the U.S. Congress—despite the fact that women were not allowed to vote until 1920.

Henry III became King of England when he was nine years old.

Air-filled tires were used on bicycles before they were used on cars.

King George I of England could not speak English.

Mexico once had three different presidents in 24 hours.

Tea is believed to have been discovered in 2737 BCE by a Chinese emperor when some tea leaves accidentally blew into a pot of boiling water.

A squirrel closed down the New York Stock Exchange one day in 1987 when it burrowed through and chewed a power line.

In ancient Egypt, certain baboons were mummified when they died.

The American army tried to train bats to drop bombs during World War II.

Sunglasses were invented by the Chinese in the thirteenth century.

Ancient Romans used urine as mouthwash.

The first e-mail was sent in 1971.

Denmark has the oldest existing national flag. The flag dates back to the thirteenth century.

Tug of War was an Olympic sport from 1900 to 1920.

It was widely believed in the Middle Ages that the heart was the center of human intelligence.

Big Ben, a clock in London, once lost four-and-a-half minutes when a group of birds used the minute hand as a perch.

Before 1600, New Year's Day was in March.

According to Aristotle, the brain's primary purpose was to cool the blood.

In the tenth century, the Grand Vizier of Persia carried his library on 400 trained camels. The camels had to walk in alphabetical order.

In ancient Japan, public contests were held to see who could fart the loudest and longest.

The story of Cinderella originated in Ancient Greece.

In ancient Egypt, men and women wore eyeshadow made from crushed beetles.

In Britain in the 1700s, dentures were sometimes made from the teeth of dead people.

In ancient Egypt, monkeys were trained to pick fruit for harvest.

Chrysler built the B-29s that bombed Japan. Mitsubishi built the Zeros that tried to shoot the B-29s down. Both companies now build cars in a joint plant called Diamond Star.

The most popular arcade game ever is Pac-Man.

The formula for cold cream was created by the Roman physician Galen.

Queen Elizabeth II of England sent her first e-mail in 1976.

In 1975, Charlie Chaplin entered a Charlie Chaplin look-alike contest and lost.

The first known labor strike occurred at the building site of an Ancient Egyptian pyramid.

The first television commercial was broadcast in 1941. It cost $9 to air.

The first TV commercial cost only $9 to air.

The oldest existing governing body, the Althing, operates in Iceland. It was established in 930 CE.

People started keeping ferrets as pets 500 years before cats were kept as pets.

In the Victorian era, it was common for people to pose and photograph loved ones after they had died.

Democracy began 2,500 years ago in Athens, Greece.

The Sumerians, who lived in the Middle East, invented the wheel in about 3450 BCE.

Leonardo da Vinci invented an alarm clock that woke you by raising your feet into the air.

In the 1400s, Christopher Columbus claimed to have seen three mermaids in the ocean during a voyage. Today it is believed they were manatees.

Long ago, thermometers were filled with brandy instead of mercury.

The first rubber balloon was invented by Michael Faraday in 1824.

The wheelbarrow was invented in ancient China.

The Olympic torch and flame were brought back by Germany for the 1936 Berlin Olympics.

The first message sent over Alexander Graham Bell's telephone on March 10, 1876 was: "Mr. Watson—come here—I want to see you."

The Romans were famous for their amazing feasts. They loved to eat exotic foods like snails, swans, crows, horses, and peacocks.

In the Philippines during the 1500s, the yo-yo was made of stone and used as a weapon.

Ancient Egyptians slept on pillows made of stone.

Bread was used as an eraser before rubber erasers were invented.

In nineteenth century Britain, you could be hung for being on a highway with a sooty face.

Since its discovery in 1930, Pluto has completed only about 20 percent of its orbit. The last time Pluto was in its present position was before the American Revolution.

Mailing an entire building has been illegal in the United States since 1916, when a man mailed a bank brick-by-brick across Utah to avoid high freight rates.

In the Tudor era, the king appointed a Master of the Stool, who was responsible for helping him go to the bathroom.

Illegal gambling houses in eighteenth-century England employed a person to swallow the dice if there was a police raid.

Ketchup was sold in the 1830s as medicine.

In *Gulliver's Travels,* Jonathan Swift described the two moons of Mars, giving their exact sizes and speeds of rotation. He did this more than 100 years before the moons were discovered.

Long ago, clans that wanted to get rid of unpopular people would burn their houses down, hence the expression "to get fired."

The word "checkmate" in chess comes from the Persian phrase "Shah Mat," which means "the king is dead."

Dentists in medieval Japan extracted teeth by pulling them out with their fingers.

Since it was against the rules to keep dogs at the college, Lord Byron kept a pet bear during his time at Cambridge instead.

Hatshepsut, the second female Pharaoh of Egypt, sometimes wore a fake beard.

Albert Einstein was offered the presidency of Israel, but turned down the job.

In 1666, the Great Fire of London burned down 13,200 houses and 87 churches.

The world's first speed limit was introduced in the United Kingdom in 1865. It was 4 miles per hour.

The first daily television broadcast began in 1936.

In nineteenth century Britain, you could be hung for stealing a spoon.

Karate originated in India, but was developed further in China.

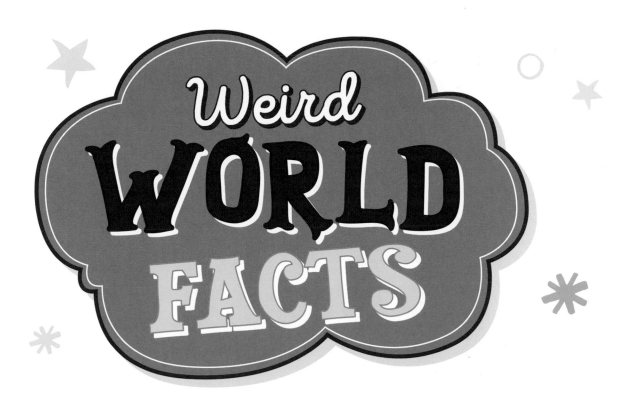

Weird WORLD FACTS

The state of Florida is larger than England.

The Earth spins at 1,000 miles per hour at the equator.

A lump of pure gold the size of a matchbox can be flattened into a sheet of gold the size of a tennis court.

Meteorites slam into the Earth every year.

The diameter of the moon is 2,159 miles.

Europe is the only continent without a major desert.

The Pacific Ocean is not as salty as the Atlantic Ocean.

Diamonds are flammable.

In Japan, there are vending machines for underwear.

In 1980, there was a traffic jam in France that was 109 miles long.

It would take a bullet fired from Earth more than 20 years to reach the Sun.

Oh great!
Somebody on Earth is doing the test to see how long it takes for a bullet to reach the Sun!

Candles burn longer when they are frozen.

The largest continent is Asia.

Microorganisms can be found as deep as 2 miles in the Earth's crust.

When it's −40°F
And there's nothing but you...the wind...and the polar bears...
You're not worried whether the South Pole is colder than the North.
IT'S ALL COLD!

The South Pole is colder than the North Pole.

The United States creates nearly 25 percent of the world's garbage.

The first living creature to orbit the Earth was a dog sent into space by Russia.

All international pilots, no matter where they are from, are required to speak English.

In a study by the University of Chicago in 1907, it was found that yellow is the easiest color to spot.

There are more chickens in the world than people.

The Greek national anthem has 158 verses.

In the Amazon rainforest, 1 sq mile can be home to 3,000 species of trees.

The moon moves 1.5 inches away from the Earth every year.

Bishop's Rock in the United Kingdom is the smallest island in the world.

A third of our water gets flushed down the toilet.

Damascus in Syria is the oldest inhabited city. It was founded in 753 BCE.

Australia is the only country that takes up an entire continent.

The British flag should only be called the Union Jack when it is on a ship at sea.

California, USA, has the fifth largest economy in the world.

More than half of the United States' coastline is in Alaska.

A storm officially becomes a hurricane when it reaches wind speeds of 74 miles per hour.

In Bangladesh, school children can be put in jail for cheating on their exams.

Half the world's population is under 25 years old.

There are about 1,800 thunderstorms occurring on Earth at any given time.

The deepest part of the Pacific Ocean is 6.8 miles.

In Australia and the United Kingdom, light switches are flicked down for on. In the United States, the switch is flicked up for on.

Every year in Sweden, a hotel is built out of ice. It melts, then it is rebuilt the next year.

The United Nations has predicted that the population of Africa will double by the year 2050.

There are more than 500,000 earthquakes throughout the world every year.

The center of the Earth is believed to be as hot as the surface of the Sun.

The most abundant metal in the ground is aluminum.

Until 1664, New York was called New Amsterdam.

The amount of water on Earth is the same now as when the planet formed 4.54 billion years ago.

Bigger raindrops make brighter rainbows.

Proportionally speaking, the Earth is smoother than a billiard ball.

Disney World in Florida is twice the size of Manhattan Island.

The Earth was supposed to be as smooth as a billiard ball... But Bob hit a rough batch over North America that sent his 9 ball right off the table.

It takes one drop of ocean water more than 1,000 years to circulate around the world.

The Earth is slightly hotter during a full moon.

Russia and America are less than 2.5 miles apart at their closest point.

There are solar-powered pay phones in the Saudi Arabian desert.

Your ears keep growing your entire life.

The international dialling code for Antarctica is 672.

Waves in the Pacific Ocean can be up to 111 ft high.

The Earth weighs 80 times more than the moon.

It takes 8 minutes and 20 seconds for light from the Sun to reach Earth.

The United States, Burma, and Liberia are the only three countries in the world to not have adopted the metric system of weights and measures.

The Amazon River pushes lots of water into the Atlantic Ocean. In fact, there is fresh water in the ocean more than 100 miles from the mouth of the river.

Eighty percent of people who are hit by lightning are men.

The average meteor is no larger than a grain of sand, but it is moving at nearly 30,000 miles per hour when it enters the atmosphere. This makes it burn so brightly that it is seen as a "shooting star" from the ground.

A raindrop falls at between 4.5 and 20 mph.

During a severe storm, the Empire State Building may give about 1.5 in on either side.

Fine-grained volcanic ash is an ingredient in some toothpastes.

A person would have to drink more than six cups of hot cocoa to consume the amount of caffeine found in one cup of coffee.

A favorite dish in old England was lark's tongue.

The pound cake got its name because the traditional recipe included one pound each of flour, sugar, butter, and eggs.

Cumin is the most popular spice in the world.

A Tanzanian dish is white ant pie.

Tanzanian white ant pie should always be eaten straight away. And never ever left out on a wooden table to cool.

The red food coloring carmine is actually made from crushed bugs.

People have been eating cheese for at least 7,500 years.

A favorite dish of Indian princes was a sparrow stuffed inside a quail stuffed inside a sandgrouse stuffed inside a chicken stuffed inside a peacock stuffed inside a goat stuffed inside a camel and roasted underground until it was tender.

Pufferfish is a Japanese delicacy, often eaten raw, but this highly toxic fish can be deadly if it is not prepared correctly.

Cultivated banana plants cannot reproduce themselves. They must be propagated by people.

The world record for the most cockroaches consumed in less than a minute is 36.

Peanuts are not actually nuts, they are legumes.

In Vietnam, there is a drink made from lizard blood.

Rat meat sausages were once a delicacy in the Philippines.

Canned food was invented in 1806, but a practical can opener was not invented until 1858.

Because Hindus do not eat beef, McDonald's in New Delhi makes lamb hamburgers.

The blue whale, the largest animal ever known to have existed, can consume 8,000 lbs of food to satisfy the massive amount of calories they must consume everyday.

Genghis Khan killed his brother after an argument over food.

The world record for eating raw eggs is six eggs in 30 seconds.

The world record for eating worms is 200 in thirty seconds.

Peanuts are one of the ingredients in dynamite.

Honey is created when bees partially digest pollen, and then throw it back up.

Rubber bands last longer when refrigerated.

A Japanese dish is broiled beetle grubs.

The annual harvest of an entire coffee plant makes 1 lb of ground coffee.

Koalas rarely drink water, as it requires them to leave their tree. Instead, they get most of their water intake from eucalyptus trees.

The first Harley Davidson motorcycle built in 1903 used a tomato can for a carburetor.

Bubble gum contains rubber.

A cure for whooping cough in old Ireland was sheep's droppings boiled in milk.

A popular dish in Belize contains mashed and roasted cockroaches.

The world record for eating snails is 144 snails in 11 minutes.

A favorite meal in China is sun-dried maggots.

Stannous fluoride, which is the cavity fighter found in toothpaste, is made from recycled tin.

Most cows give more milk when they listen to music.

More people use blue toothbrushes than red ones.

Rain contains vitamin B12.

Baked bats are served as a dish in Samoa.

A favorite dish in Mexico is lamb brain tacos.

The world record for most bananas peeled and eaten in one minute is 8.

In Ecuador, people used to eat boiled guinea pig.

The microwave was invented in the 1940s after a researcher walked by a radar tube and discovered that a chocolate bar in his pocket had melted.

Dr Austin uses the phone in front of the very same radar tube that melted his chocolate bar to tell his fellow researchers of his discovery.

Until the sixteenth century, carrots were purple, white, brown, and yellow. Then a Dutch horticulturist discovered some mutant yellow seeds that produced an orange color.

The cocoa bean was used as a currency in some ancient civilizations including the Mayan and Aztec people.

Eating an apple will make you feel more awake in the morning than drinking a cup of coffee.

Astronauts are not allowed to eat beans before they go into space because the methane released by farting in space could catch fire in spacesuits.

Most lipsticks contain fish scales.

Beef blood pudding is a favorite dish in Norway.

MOO

Erik from Norway tries out his
first beef blood pudding.

Frank Epperson invented the Popsicle when he was
11 years old.

Wonky WORD FACTS

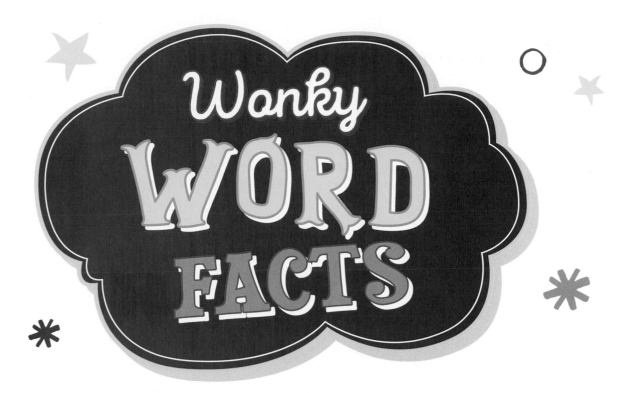

No words in the English language rhyme with month, orange, silver, or purple.

"Go" is the shortest sentence in the English language.

The word "paradise" was once the Persian word for a royal park.

The Cambodian alphabet is the largest. It has 74 letters.

The Hawaiian alphabet consists of only 15 letters.

The longest word in English is "pneumonoultramicroscopicsilicovolcanoconiosis."

Aardvark means "earth pig."

The word "SWIMS" still reads correctly when turned upside down.

The name "Jeep" comes from the abbreviation used in the army for the general purpose vehicle, GP.

The Inuit have 20 different words for snow.

Dr. Seuss invented the word "nerd."

We're often told not to run in corridors (or, hallways) these days, but the word "corridor" is actually Latin for "running place."

"Zorro" is Spanish for **"fox."**

The great Mexican superhero...Zorro

The word alphabet is made up of the first two letters in the Greek alphabet, *alpha* and *beta*.

Attics originated in Attica.

If you spelled out every number in order, you wouldn't need to use the letter "b" until you reached one billion.

"Oology" is the collection and study of eggs.

The word "diastema" means having a gap between your teeth.

The Western Gorilla's scientific name is *Gorilla gorilla*.

A *contronym* is a word that has two opposite meanings. For example, the word "cleave" can mean to cut into pieces, or to stick together.

The word "computer" was first used in 1613 to refer to a person. Before machines and computers existed, only humans could compute.

Jackie Miley of South Dakota owns 8,026 teddy bears, the world's largest collection.

The dot over the letter "i" is called the tittle.

The abbreviation "LOL," meaning "laugh out loud," has actually been added to the dictionary.

"Aloha" means both "goodbye" and "hello" in Hawaiian.

The "sixth sick sheik's sixth sheep's sick" is the toughest tongue-twister in the English language.

A baby oyster is called a spat.

The word "queueing" is the only English word with five consecutive vowels.

"The" is the most common word used in the English language.

In England in the 1880s, "pants" was considered a dirty word.

Ebineezer's wife took advantage of the London sales of Christmas 1882.
She snapped up as much cheap imported curtain material as she could find.
By turning it into pants for her husband, she gave not only him a bad name ...but PANTS a bad name as well...

A palindrome is a word or sentence that is spelled the same backward and forward. The words kayak, madam, and racecar are all palindromes.

"Of" is the only word in which an "f" is pronounced like a "v."

A pregnant goldfish is called a twit.

"Bookkeeper" and "bookkeeping" are the only words in the English language with three consecutive sets of double letters.

The word "taxi" is spelled the same in English, German, French, and Swedish.

The most used letter in the English alphabet is "e," and "z" is the least used.

The word "karaoke" means "empty orchestra."

The sentence "the quick brown fox jumps over the lazy dog" uses every letter in the alphabet.

STRANGE SCIENCE

Glass is made from sand.

Venus, the second closest planet to the sun, is by far the hottest, with an average surface temperature of 867°F.

An iceberg contains more heat than a lit match.

Velcro was invented by a person who studied the burrs that clung to his dog's coat after a walk.

White light contains the wavelengths of all the colors in the spectrum.

Leonardo da Vinci is most well-known for his paintings, but he was also a sculptor, architect, inventor, engineer, and mathematician.

Scientists are genetically engineering a breed of goat that will produce milk that can be turned into spider silk, then spun into ultra strong ropes.

Some forms of primitive life can survive anywhere that water is found, even in boiling water or ice.

The sound of a whip cracking is actually a mini sonic boom that occurs when the tip of the whip breaks the sound barrier.

Using nanotechnology, a microscopic guitar with strings has been made. It is no larger than a blood cell.

The temperature on the moon can fluctuate by up to 500°F at night.

John Logie Baird made the first television in 1924 using cardboard, scrap wood, needles, string, and other materials.

More than 1,000 new insects are discovered every year.

In 1889, the commissioner of the United States Patent Office announced that "Everything that can be invented, has been invented."

Toilet paper was invented in New York in 1857.

The first video cassette recorder was built in 1956. It was the size of an upright piano.

A cross between a goat and a sheep is called a "geep."

If a cross between a goat and sheep is a... geep. Then a cross between a dog and a pig must be... ...a dig!

The Voyager 1 spacecraft became the first man-made object to leave our solar system. It contains a time capsule with photographs and sound recordings, just in case it comes into contact with any other life forms.

At 21, inventor Thomas Edison had registered for over 1,000 patents.

The hardest naturally occurring substance on earth is a diamond. It is made completely of carbon.

Arecibo observatory in Puerto Rico has one of the largest radio telescopes in the world. It is over 1,000 ft in diameter, 167 ft deep, and covers an area of about 20 acres. It could pick up the signal from a cell phone on Jupiter.

Let's see just how well that Arecibo radio telescope works down there on Earth. I'm going to order a pizza to be delivered on this cell phone from a store in Puerto Rico.

English chemist John Walker never patented his invention of matches because he felt the idea wasn't important enough to bother.

Rainbows are formed when sunlight shines on water droplets. The colors in a rainbow always appear in the same order: red, orange, yellow, green, blue, indigo, and violet.

Plastic bottles can take around 450 years to biodegrade.

The first powered and controlled flight was achieved by Orville Wright in 1903. The flight lasted 12 seconds and traveled 120 ft.

Marie Curie was the first woman to win a Nobel Prize, and also the first woman to win two Nobel Prizes in two different categories. Her daughter, Irene, also won a Nobel Prize.

The Eiffel Tower always leans away from the Sun because heat makes the metal expand.

You can start a fire by using a lens-shaped piece of ice and concentrating a beam of sunlight onto flammable material.

The first stethoscope was made in 1816 with a roll of paper.

The electric chair was invented by a dentist.

I thought to myself... there's something about this dentist that gives me the creeps. Perhaps it was the look on his face. ...The hard uncomfortable wooden seat... the belts that tightened around me ...or the talk of exceptionally large power bills...

Cat urine glows under a black light.

Hot water freezes more quickly than cold water.

PATENT MANIA

Patent no. GB2272154 is for a ladder to enable spiders to climb out of a bath. The ladder comprises a thin, flexible strip of latex rubber that follows the inner contours of the bath. A suction pad on the ladder is attached to the top of the bath.

Patent no. GB2060081 is for a horse-powered minibus. The horse walks along a conveyor belt in the middle of the bus. This drives the wheels via a gearbox. A thermometer under the horse's collar is connected to the vehicle instrument panel. The driver can signal to the horse using a handle, which brings a mop into contact with the horse.

Patent no. GB2172200 is for an umbrella for wearing on the head. The support frame is designed not to mess up the wearer's hair.

Well...The best features of this new umbrella are that it doesn't mess up my hair... and it leaves me two hands to shop!

RAIN? Oh no... you can't use it in the rain! You'll get wet!

Patent no. GB2289222 is for a fart-collecting device. It comprised of a gas-tight collecting tube for insertion into the rectum of the subject. The tube is connected to a gas-tight collecting bag. The end of the tube inserted into the subject is covered with a gauze filter and a gas permeable bladder.

Patent no. US6325727 is for an underwater golf swing training device. The device has a hydrodynamically adjustable paddle that can be altered manually. This provides variable resistance to the user as he or she swings the device through the water.

Bob, trying out his new underwater golf swing training device, tries for the hole but only manages the side of the smimming pool.

Patent no. GB2267208 is for a portable seat that is worn on a waist-belt. The seat cushion can pivot from a stowed position to a seating position.

Patent no. US4233942 is for a device used for protecting the ears of a long-haired dog from becoming soiled by food while it is eating. A tube contains each of the dog's ears. The tubes are held away from the dog's mouth and food while it eats.

Patent no. WO9701384 is for a leash used for walking an imaginary pet. It has a preformed shape and supports a simulated pet harness and collar. A micro loudspeaker in the collar is connected to an integrated circuit in the handle, to produce a variety of barks and growls.

Patent no. GB1453920 is for rolled-up fire curtains secured at roof level on a skyscraper. When a fire starts, the curtains are released to cover the building and suffocate the fire.

Patent no. US5971829 is for a motorized ice cream cone. The cone spins while you lick the ice cream.

Rusty tried the TURBO TUTTI-FRUITY on the low setting...but wasn't getting enough tutti-fruity. So he gave it a go ...on high.

Patent no. US2760763 is for an egg beater that beats the egg within its shell.

Boy! It's cooler in this shade! But the heat must be getting to me! Where did I put my drink?

Patent no. US6637447 is for the "Beerbrella." This is a tiny umbrella that clips onto a beer bottle, keeping the sun off the beverage.

Patent no. WO98/21939 is for deer ears. To use, simply place the deer ears on your head and swivel your new ears in the direction you would like to hear.

I not only put my ears on... but like to put antlers on as well. It makes me feel like a real deer!

Sometimes I even stick a red nose on and pretend I'm Rudolph!

Patent no. US3150831 is for a birthday cake candle extinguisher.

Patent no. US5713081 is for three-legged pantyhose. When there is a run in the stocking, you simply rotate your leg into the spare hose. The damaged hose is then tucked into a pocket in the crotch of the pantyhose.

My! They certainly were three stubborn nasty little candles weren't they!

Dad gave Amelia three tries at blowing out her Birthday candles... then that was it!

Patent no. US5719656 is for earless eyewear. Stick the self-adhesive magnets onto each side of your head. The eyewear frames contain internal magnets that hold onto the magnets on your temples.

Patent no. US4022227 is for a three-way combover to cover a bald head. Just let your hair grow long at the sides, then divide it into three sections, and comb it over your bald head one section at a time.

Patent no. US4344424 is for a mouth cage that is designed to allow you to breathe and speak but not eat.

Patent no. US4872422 is for a pet petter. This is an electronic device consisting of an eye that spots your pet and signals the electronic motors to activate the petting arm. The arm is tipped with a human-like hand for added realism.

Patent no. USD342712 is for a frame that clamps around your pet's waist and supports a clear plastic tent-like structure that keeps your pet dry in the rain. There are air holes in the tent.

Patent no. US6557994 is for a way to hang eyeglasses on your face. You use body piercing studs. Pierce your eyebrows and hang your glasses from the studs. There is also a design that works with a nose bridge stud.

Patent no. US6266930 is for a "Squabble Shield." The shield is a shatterproof, clear plexiglass wall that fits in the middle of the back seat of a family car. It keeps children apart, and from squabbling, while the parent is driving.

Patent no. US4825469 is for a fully inflatable motorcycle suit. When the rider falls off the bike, the suit swells with compressed gas until it covers the head, arms, torso, and legs, protecting the rider from damage.

Patent no. US4365889 is for a wristband with an absorbent pad. People with colds can wipe their noses on it. It also has a cover that flips down, keeping all the nasties inside.

Patent no. US4299921 is for the "Smell This" breath mask. You check if your breath is smelly by placing the mask on your face, then breathing out through your mouth, and breathing in through your nose.

Patent no. US3842343 is for mud flaps to keep mud from flying up the back of your shoes.

Patent no. US6704666 is for the "Speak & Swing," which is a motorized golf club selection system. You simply speak to your golf bag, telling it which club you want, and the club automatically pops up.

Patent no. US5372954 is for the "Wig Flipper." A wig is placed on a large spring and attached to a small cap. The wig and spring are then compressed, locked onto the cap, and placed on your head. When you push the spring's release button, the hairpiece will jump into the air.

Patent no. US6600372 is for the "Spitting Duck." This device fits most toilets and, instead of using toilet paper, you lift the duck's bill, and a strategically placed nozzle will spray your bottom with the cleaning formula.

Patent no. US5352633 is for the "Arm Mitten," which the driver of a car wears on one arm. This protects the arm from sunburn when the elbow rests on the window ledge.

Patent no. US6630345 is for the "Wonder Butt Bra," which lifts, supports, and shapes a person's butt, giving it a desirable shape. It is fully adjustable to fit all sizes of butts.

Patent no. US5848443 is for the "Travel Relief." This is a padded toilet for use while driving. It even flushes.

Patent no. US5375340 is for "Cool Shoes," which are air-conditioned shoes that have a mini-network of heat exchange coils built into the heels. With each step, the wearer activates the compressor chamber, which forces cool air up into the shoe via a rubber bladder in the sole.

Patent no. US5130161 is for the "Life Expectancy Watch." You program the watch by answering questions about your lifestyle. Your estimated remaining time on Earth is displayed in years, months, days, and hours.

Every person has a unique tongue print.

Your right lung takes in more air than your left lung does.

A woman's heart beats faster than a man's.

The inventor of Vaseline ate a spoonful of the stuff every morning.

Albert Einstein never wore socks.

Astronauts get taller when they are in space.

People photocopying their butts is the cause of 23 percent of all photocopier malfunctions.

It is impossible to cry in space because of the lack of gravity.

No two humans have the same fingerprint.

Less than one percent of bacteria are harmful to humans.

In low temperatures, your extremities (hands, feet, nose, and ears) will get cold first, because your body concentrates on sending blood to your vital organs.

Most people produce about a cupful of snot every day.

When you go down the steep slope of a roller coaster, the harness holds you in place but some of your internal organs move around. Your nerves sense this movement, which is what causes the "free fall" feeling in your stomach.

There are four basic tastes the human tongue can detect. Salty and sweet are tasted on the tip of the tongue, bitter is tasted at the base of the tongue, and sour is tasted along the sides of the tongue.

The average person blinks between 15–20 times per minute.

Albert Einstein's eyes were kept by his eye doctor and are still being stored in a safety deposit box since his death in 1955. They are rumored to be poised for auction.

Wedding rings are worn on the fourth finger of the left hand because people used to believe that the vein in this finger goes directly to the heart.

Human dreams can last up to thirty minutes.

25 percent of your bones are located in your feet.

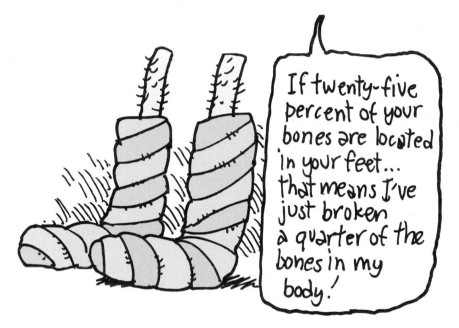

The numbers of births in India each year exceeds the entire population of Australia.

The world's human population was only five million in 5000 BCE.

If the population of China lined up and you had to walk the length of the line, you would be walking forever because of all the new births.

Artist Stephen Wiltshire drew an 18-foot picture of New York City from memory after flying over the city in a helicopter for only 20 minutes.

The measurement from your wrist to your elbow in inches is the same measurement as your shoe size.

Over 10 percent of American households dress their pets in Halloween costumes.

Arteries carry blood away from the heart. Veins carry blood toward the heart.

According to a study by the Economic Research Service, 27 percent of all food produced in Western nations ends up in garbage cans. Yet 1.2 billion people in the world are underfed.

Girls have more taste buds than boys do.

There are only about 100 commonly used family names in China for a population of well over a billion.

You breathe in and out up to 30,000 times a day.

The average height of people in Western nations has increased by 4 inches in the last 150 years.

Your stomach acid can dissolve metal.

One out of 200 people has an extra rib.

Research has shown that old people have a different—and more pleasant—smell than young and middle-aged people.

New Zealand was the first country to give women the right to vote.

The average person has from 4 to 6 dreams per night.

A corpse exposed to insects and elements can be reduced to a skeleton in a matter of days.

The most common name in the world is Mohammed.

Roald Dahl was buried with chocolate as an ode to *Charlie and the Chocolate Factory.*

Color blindness is more common in men than in women.

Taste buds last about ten days. Of course, your body is making new ones all the time.

In India in the early 90s, people wore masks on the back of their heads when they went outside. This was meant to confuse tigers because they like to attack from the rear.

Humans spend one third of their lives sleeping.

Robots in Japan pay union dues.

Author Ernest Vincent Wright wrote an entire novel, called *Gadsby*, without the letter "e."

All babies are color blind when they are born.

Boanthropy is a disease that makes a person believe he or she is an ox.

A person cannot taste food unless it is mixed with saliva. For example, if salt is placed on a dry tongue, the taste buds will not be able to taste it. As soon as a drop of saliva is added and the salt is dissolved, the person tastes the salt.

The Beijing Duck Restaurant in China can seat 5,000 people.

Tibetans and Mongolians put salt and butter in their tea instead of sugar.

The average person farts enough each day to fill a party balloon.

There are about a trillion nerves at work in your brain that relate to memory.

Maasai tribesmen from Tanzania do not bury their dead because they respect the earth and believe burial is harmful to the soil.

There are villages in Papua New Guinea that are only a 20-minute walk apart, but the villagers speak different languages.

The Neanderthal's brain was bigger than your brain is.

A pair of leather shoes can supply enough nourishment for a person for about a week.

Napoleon Bonaparte's penis was put up for auction and sold in 1977.

A human liver can grow back if part of it is removed.

The Inuit use fridges to stop their food from freezing.

The only part of the human body that has no blood supply is the cornea of the eye. It takes in oxygen directly from the air.

Fingernails live for three to six months. They grow nearly 1.5 inches a year.

A 4 inch lock of Beethoven's hair was up for auction at Sotheby's for $4,600 in 2015.

There is a 50 percent chance that a child born by two parents with dwarfism will also have the condition.

Forty percent of dog and cat owners carry pictures of their pets in their wallets.

One in four Americans think the Sun orbits the Earth.

Your sense of smell is about five percent as strong as a dog's.

Human skin sheds continually. The outer layer of skin is entirely replaced every 28 days.

An adult human has 32 teeth.

In Los Angeles, there are more cars than people.

A person's arm span measures roughly the same as their height.

The body of Charlie Chaplin was stolen in 1978 from a Swiss graveyard and held for ransom. The sum demanded was 600,000 francs.

Rowan Atkinson, who plays Mr. Bean and Johnny English, has a Master's Degree in Electrical Engineering.

Manhole covers are always round because they rest on a lip that is smaller than the cover. This means the cover cannot fit through the opening on any angle. A square or rectangular cover could fall through.

Gavin's head was square. So he found it difficult to fit through round manholes.

BONK
BUMP
CLUNK

Studies show that in the United States, deaf people have safer driving records than people who can hear.

The stapes is the smallest bone in the human body. It is found in the ear.

Sweat doesn't smell bad—it's actually the bacteria that lives on your skin and feeds on your sweat that creates body odor.

Every human shares more than 99 percent of their DNA with every other person.

On average, men sweat more than women do.

The hardest substance in the human body is tooth enamel.

Most adults will grow to roughly twice the height they were at age two.

Some people have a condition that causes them to mix up senses so that they can taste sounds or hear colors. It is called synesthesia.

Sixty percent of Americans urinate in the shower.

The human heart pumps around 800,000 gallons of blood throughout the body each year.

The average person laughs 15 times a day.

Chinese people make up more than 20 percent of the world's population.

The largest cell in the human body is the ovum, the female reproductive cell.

Scientists believe that our fingers become pruney when they are wet in order to help them grip wet objects.

The longest beard on a woman was 10 inches.

The condition where a person has two different-colored eyes is called heterochromia.

The most prolific mother gave birth to a total of 69 children.

In Albania, nodding your head means no and shaking it means yes.

While asking an Albanian lady for directions Austin is unaware that in Albania people shake their heads for yes.. and nod for no. Austin ends up in neighboring Serbia instead of the Airport.

While you are reading this sentence, 50,000 cells in your body will have been replaced by new cells.

Human cells are so small that around 10,000 could fit on the head of a pin.

Although an extremely rare occurrence, sneezing too hard can fracture a rib.

The human brain is already 90 percent of its full size by the time a child is six.

The oldest known person lived to 122 years of age.